DATE			

Market research, 193–212, 221
Market segmentation, 207–208, 221–222
Market selection, 221–222
Market shakeout, 554
Market share, 92, 118, 137–139, 206, 521, 540
"Market skimming" strategy, 226
Marketing, 16, 83–87, 101–102, 114, 140, 206–207, 219, 222, 233, 235, 313, 570
Marketing information system, 493–494
Marketing strategies, 69–70, 207–212, 236–237
Marketplace challenge, 153–154, 191–192
Marketplace opportunity, 158–159
Master general agent, 209
Maternity care, 68, 110, 154, 187, 350, 385, 389–390, 524, 555, 575
Matrix management, 229
Maxicare Health Plan, 127, 137
Maximum fee level, 302–303
MCIS (*see* Managed care information system)
MDC (*see* Major Diagnostic Category)
MedFacts, 534–536
Medicaid, 30, 68, 447–448, 553, 557–574, 584
 cost of, 559
 future trends in, 564–565, 572–573
 impact of process requirements, 570–572
 limitations on, 571–573
 locus of risk in, 562–563
 monitoring of, 569–570
 participation requirements, 568–569
 populations and services covered, 563–564
 priorities, 574
 rate setting, 565–568
 voluntary vs. mandatory participation, 560–562
Medicaid Healthcare Initiative (Oregon), 576–578
Medical audit, 424
Medical expense report, 329–330
Medical licensing board, 373
Medical necessity, 22, 108, 110, 163, 170, 191, 266, 354, 459, 541, 558, 586
Medical records, 156, 225, 426, 435–437, 482, 488
Medical records review, 380–384, 397, 588
Medical staff-hospital organization (PHO), 141
Medicare, 30, 33, 68, 447–448, 553, 557–573, 584
 cost of, 559
 future trends in, 564–565, 572–573
 impact of process requirements, 570–572
 limitations on, 571–573
 locus of risk in, 562–563
 monitoring of, 569–570
 participation requirements, 568–569
 populations and services covered, 563–564
 rate setting, 565–568
 supplementary benefits, 158, 561
 violations, 167
 voluntary vs. mandatory participation, 560–562
Medicare Fee Schedule, 366–367
Medicare Insured Group, 561
Medisgroups, 381, 415
"Memberless" taxable nonprofit corporation, 249, 252–253, 257–260
Mental healthcare, 39, 121, 153, 164, 168, 171, 183, 185, 189–190, 238–241, 268, 276, 339, 349, 353, 385, 516–517, 524, 563
Merger, 237
MET (*see* Multiple employer trust)
Mission statement, 215–216, 427, 432
Monopoly or conspiracy in restraint of trade, 256
Mortality statistics, 424, 427
Multipatient data profiling, 380–382
Multiple employer trust (MET), 209
Multiple-option plan, 332
Multiple per diem schedule, 163
Multiple shareholder professional corporation, 249, 251
MYCIN, 475

National Medicare Competition Evaluation, 567
Negotiating styles, 126–128, 136–141
Negotiating tactics, 5, 13–16, 137–142
Negotiating team, 127, 131–132
Negotiation objectives, 128–131, 134–140, 299
Negotiation site, 132–133
Negotiations, 124–147, 314, 491
 antitrust constraints on, 43–45
 conduct of, 132–134
 from managed plan's perspective, 134–138
 preparation for, 128–134, 142–143
 from provider's perspective, 138–140
 records of, 133–134
 written proposal for, 134
Neonatal care (*see* Infant care)
Network development, 166–170
Network rental arrangement, 178
Neutral negotiator, 137

New England Medical Center, 144-147
New patient codes, 390, 392
New products, 187-188
No coverage option, 278
Noncontrollable services, 350, 353
Norms, 462-463, 470, 476, 510, 521
Nursing care, 70, 155, 186, 405-410, 553-554
Nursing home care, 185, 555, 558-559, 563
Nutritional services, 190, 576, 578

Objective negotiator, 141
OBRA (*see* Omnibus Budget Reconciliation Act)
Observation unit, 406-407, 411
Occupational medicine, 165-166
Occupational nurse, 111, 285
Occupational therapy, 155, 576
Office of Prepaid Health Care, 32
Office visit, 162, 181, 274, 283, 311-312, 375, 391, 517-518, 522, 540, 559
Offset error, 468
Omnibus Budget Reconciliation Act (OBRA, 1981), 27
One-line data processing, 486
One-stop shopping, 152-153, 164, 221
Open-access care product, 306
Open-ended options, 178
Open enrollment, 87
Operating costs, 254
Operations data, 484-485
Opinion leader interviews, 198
Opt-out product, 298
Oregon Medicaid priorities, 574-576
Organ transplant, 109-110, 145, 554, 576
Organization goals, 215-216
Organizational structure, 154, 219, 243-263
Out-of-area services, 88, 155, 272, 350
Out-of-compliance notice, 487
Out-of-network services, 34, 38, 152, 181, 189, 234, 271-273, 279, 353, 358, 364-365, 547
Out-of-pocket costs, 62-63, 66, 118, 189, 195, 267-268, 275, 532, 534
Outliers, 147, 157, 352-353, 423, 427, 467, 472, 588
Outpatient care, 162, 164, 168, 183-185, 190, 223-224, 261, 347-348, 357-359, 381, 406-411, 529-530, 540, 558
Outpatient data, 520, 524
Outpatient surgery, 155, 347-348, 390, 394-399
Overhead, 115, 355
Overpayment, 448
Overtreatment, 467
Overutilization, 398-399
Ownership, 180

Package pricing, 83, 164
Partnership approach, 13, 14, 550
Patient (*see* Consumer *entries*; Patient *entries*)
Patient accounting system, 488
Patient attitudes, 382
Patient behavior, 80, 461-462
Patient education, 382
Patient flow, 92-93
Patient grievance, 532
Patient health status, 12-13
Patient information, 483
Patient satisfaction, 8-13, 365
Patient scheduling, 225
Patient volume, 85, 126, 137, 139, 144-145, 223, 314-315, 320-321, 334-335, 355, 365, 480
Patterns of Treatment, 379-380, 462, 530
Payer, government as, 30-32
Payer perspective, 19-20, 89-104
Payment audit, 487, 492
Payment controls, 551
Payment cycle, 464
Payment date, 463-464
Payment system, 183-184
  ancillary services, 347-354
  hospital, 342-343
  physician, 335-342, 366-367
Peer grouping, 398
Peer review, 153, 255-257, 367, 373, 424, 588
Penalty provision, 268
Pension plan, 245-253
Per case payments, 223
Per claimant measures, 522
Per confinement deductibles, 268
Per diems, 135, 145-146, 156-157, 163, 184, 223, 237, 344, 347, 350-351, 362
Per employee per month fee, 163
Per stay reimbursement, 344-345, 352-353
Percent-of-pay cost sharing, 268
Performance agreement, 527-528
Performance appraisal, 227
Performance by contract, 487
Performance by service, 487
Performance guarantee, 24, 83
Performance scoring system, 399
Performance standards, 8-13, 158-159, 424, 540, 549-550, 588
Performance targets, 355
PHO (*see* Medical staff-hospital organization)
Physical therapy, 155, 190, 576
Physician (*See also* Provider *entries*)
  company, 111
  out-of-plan, 28-29
Physician attitudes, 58-67, 78, 82-83, 95, 377-378
Physician education, 373-374, 391-392, 396, 425, 471-472
Physician elimination, 257, 392, 396-397
Physician Payment Review Commission, 366-367

Physician payment system, 335–342, 366–367
Physician review, 78–79
Physician staff office system, 488
Physician survey, 534
Piggyback system, 484
Plan design, 161–162, 181–183, 188–189, 267–275
Plan penetration, 161
Planning, 94–95, 199
Pluralism, 53, 554
Podiatry, 39, 164, 168, 171, 186, 268, 385, 576
Point-of-service plan, 38–39, 152, 178, 181, 266, 270–271, 278, 283, 547
Population-based analysis, 505–506
PPA (preferred provider arrangement), 31, 35–37
PPO (*see* Preferred provider organization)
PPS (*see* Prospective Payment System)
Practice norms, 462
Practice pattern, 79, 82, 107, 144, 153, 157, 270, 293, 304, 335–336, 355, 366, 390, 392, 411, 448, 454, 505–506, 548, 566, 587–588
Practice standards, 333, 367, 419, 462, 529
Preadmission center, 411–413
Preadmission certification, 21, 26, 42, 109, 185, 189, 268, 321, 393–395, 402
Preadmission interview, 485
Preadmission review, 21, 224, 558
Preadmission screening, 80, 185, 345, 406–407, 411
Preauthorization, 484, 486
Preferred Health Network, 207–212, 237
Preferred provider contracting, 177
Preferred provider organization (PPO), 3, 80–83, 87–88, 160–170, 182, 266, 332, 571, 582–583
  benefit design, 274–275
  claims data, 521–523
  employer-controlled, 369–370
  finances of, 346–347
  first generation, 539
  marketing strategies for, 207–212
  Medicare, 561–562
  national, 85, 160
  physician-owned, 243–260
  regional, 160
  second generation, 539
  third generation, 539–540
Preferred provider panel, 45
Pregnancy (*see* Maternity care)
Premiums, 33–34, 88, 96, 131, 239, 280, 333, 365, 523, 587
Prenatal care (*see* Maternity care)
Prepaid health plan, 569–571
Prepayment review, 394–396
Prescription drugs, 154–155, 164, 171, 205, 223–224, 267, 274–275, 283, 312, 348–349, 380, 516, 532, 549, 563, 576
Preservice review, 376
Preventative Health Account, 285–286
Preventative care (*see* Wellness program)
Price, 116, 548
Price competition, 74, 233
Price-fixing, 44–45, 258
Price sensitivity, consumer, 195–197
Pricing, 74–75, 97–99, 163, 225–226, 237, 279–280, 287–320, 532–533 (*See also specific types of pricing*)
Primary care, 74, 86–87
Primary care capitation, 339–340, 359–363
Primary care case management, 563
Primary care physician, 74, 316, 322, 449, 454
Principled negotiations, 128
Prior authorization, 156–157, 261, 355, 402, 448, 454–460, 476, 558
Prior review, 396
Privacy concerns, 476
Private Healthcare Systems, 85
Private review agent (*see* Utilization management company)
PRO (*see* Professional Review Organization)
Problem formulation, 434
Problem-oriented medical record, 434–437
Procedures codes, 456, 526
Process control, 418
Process improvement, 425–433
Product differentiation, 224, 237, 540
Product diversification, 176–177
Product offering, 220–221
Product positioning, 193–212
Productivity assumptions, 210–211
Professional autonomy, 384
Professional corporation, 250–251, 257
Professional partnership, 249–250
Professional Review Organization (PRO), 558
Profitable operation, 95
Program enhancement research, 205
Program specialization, 23
Progress report, 219
Project team, 430
Prompt payment discount, 40
Prospective fee negotiations, 186
Prospective payment, 72, 422–423
Prospective Payment System (PPS), 557
Prospective review, 356, 585
Provider (*See* Hospital *entries*; Physician *entries*; Provider *entries*)
Provider assessment, 299
Provider attitudes, 58–67, 103, 365

Provider behavior, 451-452, 467-469
Provider contracts, 42, 238
Provider differentiation, 197
Provider exclusion, 46
Provider fees, 257-259
Provider income, 66, 137-139, 302-304, 315
Provider information, 446-447, 453-454
Provider network, 14, 16, 81, 92, 166-168, 192, 219-223, 236, 238, 521-523
Provider panel, 134-136, 255-256
Provider performance, 6, 72, 241, 302, 485
Provider perspective, 71-88, 138-140, 314-317, 548-551
Provider profile, 22-23, 81-82, 157, 161, 165-168, 380-382, 392-399, 449, 455, 460, 462, 467-471, 487, 492-493, 529, 536, 540
Provider recruitment, 223
Provider selection, 82, 85, 166-168, 270, 372-373, 391-392, 396-397, 414, 541
Provider strategies, 480
Provider termination, 82, 322, 372
Psychiatric care, 153, 155, 158, 161, 171, 183-190, 223, 268, 274, 349, 549, 576
Public health, 555, 568, 589
Public hospital, 579
Public opinion, 51-68, 90, 422, 559-560
Public policy, 51, 194
Purchaser (*see* Employer *entries*; Purchaser *entries*)
Purchaser attitudes, 16-19, 83-84, 103
Purchaser behavior, 451-452
Purchaser-oriented care report, 441-443
Purchaser perspective, 105-123, 317-319, 549-551
Purchaser requirements, 118
Purchasing decisions, 18, 107, 120-121

QHP (*see* Qualified health plans)
Qualified health plans (QHP), 553
Quality, 56-58, 70, 116-117
  definition of, 108, 416-418, 432, 434
  perceived, 135
Quality assessment, 9-11, 79, 106-109, 114, 117, 424, 528-529
Quality assurance, 6-13, 22, 49, 114, 136, 140, 156, 165, 176, 219, 223-224, 321, 401-419, 423-427, 431, 531-533, 540, 585
Quality control, 10-11, 113-115, 421-437
Quality improvement, 10-11, 114, 417-419, 431-433
Quality improvement theory, 425-430
Quality management, 469-473
Quality planning, 418
Quality specifications, 118

Radiology, 360, 423, 482, 517, 522, 583
Rate guarantee, 183, 318
Rate setting, 40-41, 565-568
Rationing, 554, 586, 589
Recap, 210
Recredentialing, 241
Referrals, 42, 80, 86, 122, 156-157, 270-274, 357-361, 363, 398, 455, 459, 461, 565
Regional healthcare management, 120-121
Regulation, 5, 25, 41, 48-49, 552
  federal, 28-32
  state, 32-41, 48-49, 98, 166, 275
Rehabilitation, 108-109, 164, 168, 184, 190, 223, 407-410, 415, 578
Reimbursement, 14-15, 156-157, 163-164, 181-182, 287-320, 354-356, 461, 473-474, 480-485, 529, 557-560, 572-574, 577
  incentive-based, 10
  trends in, 25-26
Reimbursement accuracy, 490
Reimbursement audit, 489
Reimbursement level, 565-566
Reimbursement methodologies, 331-357, 542
Reimbursement penalty, 540
Reimbursement predictability, 135-136, 139
Reimbursement rates, 85, 128, 131, 135-136, 139, 142, 145, 522
Reimbursement strategy, 6, 43-45, 122, 125-126, 299, 301-302
Reinsurance, 156
Relative value scale, 163, 299-300, 367
Renegotiation, 136, 139, 492
Renewal, 52, 62-63, 529
Replacement product, 306
Report, 486-488
Report design, 473-475
Reporting, 461-469, 485, 540, 542
Required data, 525-526
Research agenda, 581-590
Reserve requirement, 33
Resource development, 94-95
Resource requirements, 218-219
Resource use, 22
Retiree health benefits, 68, 224, 283, 552
Retirement plan (*see* Pension plan)
Retrospective review, 21, 185, 190, 224, 356, 376, 394, 558, 585
Return-to-work, 11, 108-109
Revenues, 95
Risk, 287-320
Risk analysis, 216
Risk contract, 83, 422

Risk management, 111–113, 166, 219–220, 354–356
Risk-pooling, 334–335
Risk-profile analysis, 511
Risk-sharing, 14, 37, 93, 156–157, 161, 244, 306–311, 319, 321, 529, 548, 550, 562–563
Risk transfer, 8, 314–318, 335, 341–342, 346, 354, 480, 510, 525
Rutland Regional Medical Center, 505–506
Ryder System, Inc. (Miami, FL), 534–536

SAFECO/United Healthcare, 372, 374
St. Clair Hospital (Pittsburgh, PA), 417–419
Sales, 96–97
Sales force, 211–212, 219, 222, 236, 570
Savings, 316, 468, 572, 582
Science-based managed care, 393
Second opinion, 80, 162, 185–186, 190, 224, 265, 268–269, 376, 378, 402, 459
Secondary payer, 458
Securities laws, 252
Select Care, 73, 75, 77, 80–83
SELECT Health, 235–237
Select Provider Program, 122–123
Selective contracting, 109–110, 123
Self-insureds, 209–210, 237
Self-referral options (SRO), 48–49
Senior management, 227–230, 236, 452
Service date, 463–464
Service requirements, 99
Service specifications, 106–107
Service standards, 106–107
Service terms, 136
Services, 225, 541
  of EPO, 158
  of HMO, 155–156
  of insurance company, 184
  of IPA, 156–157
  ordered vs. performed, 398
  of PPO, 160–161
  of URO, 171–176
Severity of illness, 5, 147, 165, 351, 377, 381, 404, 424, 456, 469–470, 474, 505–506, 515
  measurement of, 415–416, 474
Severity of Illness Index, 381
Shadow pricing, 29, 154, 319, 582
Sherman Act, 44–46
Shewhart cycle, 430
Shock losses, 304
Simulation, 487, 491, 493
Single-service plan, 39–40
Site license, 489
Site of care, 162, 265, 450, 558, 588
Situation analysis, 214, 217
Small area analysis, 381
Smaller community, 320–321
Smart card, 96
Social change, 51–53
Social science, applied, 477
Social services, 564
Software, 488–489, 540
Sole shareholder professional corporation, 249, 251, 253, 257, 259
Southern California Edison Co., 285–286
Special variance, 434
Specialty care, 74, 110, 135, 158, 164, 167, 174–175, 184, 222, 454–455
Speech therapy, 155, 190, 576
Spend-down case, 563
Spreadsheet, 483, 521, 523
SRO (*see* Self-referral options)
Stand-alone services, 158, 164–165
Standards of care, 82, 112, 462–463, 539
Start-up costs, 253–254
State regulations, 32–41, 48–49, 98, 166, 275
Stop-loss protection, 304, 318, 352–353, 562
Strategic decisions, 490
Strategic management assessment, 230–231
Strategic options, 220–227
Strategic partners, 226–227
Strategic plan, 213–241, 483
Strategy development, 214–217
Strategy implementation, 214, 219
Strategy retreat, 214, 218
Subcontracting, 226
Substance abuse treatment, 153, 155, 158, 161, 171, 183–190, 223, 238–241, 268, 276, 312, 349, 353, 516–517, 524, 549, 576
Summa Health Plan, 261–263
Surgery package fees, 389–390
Surgical review, 190
Systems analysis, 425
Systems integration, 171

Target market, 222
Task force, 218
Tax Equity and Fiscal Responsibility Act (TEFRA, 1982), 27
Taxable nonprofit corporation, 245, 249–253, 257, 259
TEFRA (*see* Tax Equity and Fiscal Responsibility Act)
Telephone survey, 200–204, 322–329
Tenneco Inc., 122–123
Tertiary care, 74–75, 144–147, 157, 355, 369, 407, 454–455
Third-generation managed care, 539–543
Third party administrator (TPA), 156, 188–192, 208, 210, 222, 236, 492, 549, 551

Third party payment, 447
TPA (*see* Third party administrator)
Tracer diagnoses, 462, 473
Trade-offs, 4–8, 103, 135, 551, 574
Training program, 95–96, 101
Treatment analysis, 10–11
Treatment decisions, 79–80, 179
Treatment decisions, 79–80, 179
Treatment options, 5, 179–180
Treatment outcome, 8–12, 22–23, 70, 108, 110, 119, 122, 237, 276, 393, 425, 427, 529, 540–541, 574, 585–588
Treatment plan, 146, 240–241, 435
Trend analysis, 464
Triaging, 159, 411–414, 425
Triple options, 37–39, 88, 152, 158, 182
Trust funds, 550

Unbundling, 395
Underwriting, 96–98, 157, 318, 509–510
Uninsureds, 90, 553–554, 559, 579
Unions, 208–210
Unit costs, 355
Universe, 210
Unnecessary procedure, 5, 115, 166
UR (*see* Utilization review)
URO (*see* Utilization review organization)
"Usual, customary and reasonable" charges, 183, 560
Utilization control, 80, 238–239, 314, 333
Utilization criteria, 240–241
Utilization data, 508–525, 532
Utilization level, 311–312, 315–316
Utilization management, 8, 20–24, 78–79, 108–109, 136, 140, 153, 159, 161, 165–169, 192, 219, 223–224, 271, 288, 371–386, 394–399, 404–413, 540–541
  barriers to, 383–384
  future trends in, 385–386, 413–414
  methods of, 372–382
Utilization management company, 41–42, 224
Utilization monitoring, 492, 515
Utilization rate, 289–291
Utilization report, 513–514, 522
Utilization review (UR), 6, 20–24, 79–80, 102, 108–112, 145–146, 153–159, 163–169, 177, 184–189, 240, 259, 261, 271, 276, 317, 321, 345, 364, 370, 401–414, 448, 459–460, 468, 540, 585, 587
  bundle or unbundle, 185
  impact of, 378–379
  ingredients in, 376–378
  methods of, 402–404
  physician hostility to, 377–378
  reviewer characteristics, 376–377
  supportive benefit plan for, 378
  system integrity, 377
  techniques of, 371–399
Utilization review organization (URO), 168–177, 470
Utilization review program, 85, 526–527
Utilization review service, 458
Utilization standards, 355, 377–378
Utilization trends, 443, 522

Value research, 193
Vantage Direct, 240–241
Variance, 434
Variance days, 404–411
Vendor-driven planning, 496–497
Vision care, 39, 154, 164, 184, 223–224, 283, 339, 353, 576
"Vital few and trivial many" concept, 465–467
Volume-dependent measures, 398
Voucher system, 561

Wellness program, 5, 68, 92, 107, 111–112, 184, 191, 274, 283, 285, 549, 575, 582–583, 588
Whip sawing, 138
Windowing, 493
Withholds, 181, 302, 306–310, 316, 321, 337–342, 359–363, 474, 529
Workers compensation, 161, 164–166, 171, 174, 177, 184, 186, 208, 222–224, 549

Xerox Corp. (Stamford, CT), 118–119